Table of Contents

Introduction

T0123829

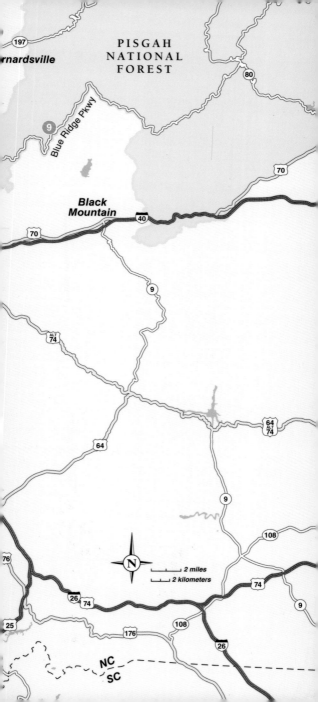

Introduction

Asheville has a lot to offer outdoors enthusiasts. The city is pleasantly walkable, with distinctive architecture and public spaces. It sits on the French Broad River, which is perfect for tubing and paddling. The surrounding mountains provide not only a dramatic setting but also thousands of trails, which lead to endless summit vistas and gorgeous waterfalls. The Blue Ridge Parkway offers road cyclists a scenic and lung-busting ride, while mountain bikers can explore the singletrack and gravel roads of Pisgah and DuPont forests for days.

Asheville's parks, gardens, and conservancies make the diverse natural beauty of the Southern Appalachians more accessible. You can spend an afternoon in the backwoods with a guided fishing trip or horseback ride. And if you're looking for an adrenaline rush, check out the whitewater rafting, zipline and canopy tours, climbing walls, bike parks, and more.

Whatever your taste in outdoor fun, Asheville has it all—plus a thriving local arts, food, and craft brew scene when you're ready to relax.

Although many of the locations featured in this book are suitable for multiple outdoors activities, if the area is especially known for one or two specific pursuits, we've listed them on the page using the indicators that you see to the right.

HIKING
BIKING
PADDLING
ZIPLINING

Covered bridge above High Falls, DuPont State Forest

ADVENTURE CENTER OF ASHEVILLE

BIKING
ZIPLINING

If you're in the mood for adrenaline, head here; you'll find several active outdoor possibilities less than 3 miles from Pack Square.

Difficulty: Moderate to Difficult, depending on the activities/routes you choose

Length/Time: Varies by activity; at least 2 hours

Hours/Fees: Open year-round; Hours and fees vary by activity

Getting There: *1 Resort Dr.* GPS: N35° 35.6678', W82° 34.8056'

Contact: 828-225-2921; ashevilletreetopsadventurepark.com

Additional Information: Kolo Bike Park includes approximately 4 miles of mountain bike trails. The rolling terrain features wooded singletrack, a flow trail, bridges, berms, balance features, dirt jumps, and two pump tracks. The trails are suitable for all skill levels, and you can rent a bike on-site or bring your own. Helmets (available to rent) and closed-toed shoes are required.

A treetop challenge course with five trails (from beginner to challenging) presents more than 60 climbing, jumping, swinging, and rappelling options for ages 4 and older. A 3-hour zipline canopy tour includes 11 ziplines and three sky bridges. There's also a 2-hour tour, a smaller zipline tour just for kids, and a free-fall "quick jump." In fact, this is a great spot to get youngsters outdoors for a birthday party.

The Adventure Center is located within a designated tree preserve, which contains some of the oldest and biggest oaks in Asheville. While among the trees on the challenge course or the ziplines, you'll enjoy some wonderful views of Asheville's skyline and the surrounding mountains.

Take a free, self-guided tour of downtown Asheville's history, architecture, and public sculptures.

Difficulty: Moderate

Length/Time: 2 miles; 2 hours

Hours/Fees: 24 hours; Free

Getting There: Begin at the intersection of Patton Ave. and Biltmore Ave. in downtown Asheville. GPS: N35° 35.6961', W82° 33.1165'

Contact: A map of the Asheville Urban Trail, with information about points of interest along the route, is available at ashevillenc.gov/parks. For more information, visit the Asheville Information Center at the Pack Square Park Pavilion in Pack Square Park.

Additional Information: Hilly terrain makes this stroll through the city a surprisingly good workout. The trail includes 30 stops, beginning and ending at the edge of Pack Square Park, named after timber magnate George Willis Pack, in the heart of the city. Along the way, you'll learn about famous past residents of Asheville, including authors O. Henry and Thomas Wolfe; Dr. Elizabeth Blackwell, who founded the first four-year medical college for women; 1800s influential politician Zebulon Baird Vance, for whom the Vance Monument is named; and patent-medicine millionaire Edwin Wiley Grove. ♿

Asheville is celebrated for its Art Deco architecture. The tour takes you past two of the best examples, the Asheville City Building and the S&W Building. Other important structures on the tour include Asheville's first "skyscraper," the Jackson Building, the Grove Arcade, and the Basilica of St. Lawrence. The Basilica (97 Haywood St.) is open to the public, and it's worth the detour to look inside.

BEAVER LAKE BIRD SANCTUARY AND LAKE VIEW PARK

A 10-minute drive from Asheville's central square is the best place in the city for bird-watching.

Difficulty: Easy

Length/Time: Approximately 1 mile; 1-1.5 hours

Hours/Fees: Sunrise-sunset daily; Free, except: Fishing permit (with valid North Carolina fishing license), $5; Annual fishing, boating, or dog-walking permit, $50

Getting There: From downtown, head north on Broadway to Merrimon Ave. for 2.8 miles. The entrance to the bird sanctuary is on the left, just past the North Asheville Library. A second parking area is past Beaver Lake, on the left. Bird Sanctuary GPS: N35° 38.0154', W82° 33.4334'; Park GPS: N35° 38.3307', W82° 33.7626'

Contact: thelakeviewpark.org and emasnc.org/beaverlake.html

Additional Information: Scenic, 65-acre Beaver Lake is open to fishing. You may rent a boat on-site, but swimming is not allowed. A mostly paved, level walking path—popular with joggers and dog-walkers—follows a portion of the lake's shoreline. Beyond Beaver Lake lies the historic Lakeview Park neighborhood, planned in the 1920s by landscape architect John Nolen, a student of Frederick Law Olmsted. ♿

The 10-acre Beaver Lake Bird Sanctuary is half uplands and half wetlands habitat. A 0.4-mile boardwalk loop explores the area. Bird-watchers will see the greatest variety of species in late spring and early summer, and again from late summer to October.

There are no restrooms at Lake View Park or the bird sanctuary. Pets are not allowed in the bird sanctuary. Leashed pets are allowed in Beaver Lake Park, by permit.

A 6,000-acre site within Pisgah National Forest, Bent Creek is the main getaway for many local hikers and cyclists.

Difficulty: Moderate to Difficult, depending on the trails you choose

Length/Time: Up to 40 miles of trails; at least 2 hours

Hours/Fees: Sunrise-sunset daily; Free

Getting There: *1577 Brevard Rd.* GPS: N35° 30.2655', W82° 35.7879'

Contact: srs.fs.usda.gov/bentcreek/

Additional Information: From downtown Asheville, take I-240W to I-26E, to Exit 33 (NC 191). Turn left at the light and continue 2 miles to Bent Creek Ranch Rd., on the right. Continue just over a mile: A sign marks the entrance to the forest. The first of several parking areas (Rice Pinnacle) is on the right.

The trails in Bent Creek vary from smooth and flowing to rocky, rooted, and technical. Climbs are frequent and can be steep, but few are sustained. Generally, the trails become more challenging as you ascend (elevations range 2,000-4,100 feet).

With a few well-marked exceptions, all trails are open to all users in either direction. Green's Lick Trail provides the ultimate descent—and the longest climb—for mountain bikers. Intermediate and advanced riders will also enjoy Upper and Lower Sidehill, Explorer Loop, and Ingles Field Gap trails.

Service roads and trails are labeled at many intersections; however, a trail map is recommended. Trail maps for Bent Creek can be found at many local bookstores, bike shops, and outfitters.

BILTMORE ESTATE

Famous for the Biltmore House, a vast, châteauesque mansion, the Biltmore Estate has much to offer nature lovers, as well.

Difficulty: Easy to Difficult, depending on the activities/routes you choose

Length/Time: Up to 22 miles of hiking trails; routes of any length available; plan to spend at least half a day at the estate.

Hours/Fees: Hours vary by season, but the main gate typically opens at 8:30 a.m. Hiking and biking available year-round; Per person, $50-$75, plus additional costs for equipment rentals and guided activities

Getting There: *1 Lodge St.* GPS: N35° 32.4340', W82° 33.1392'

Contact: 800-411-3812; biltmore.com

Additional Information: The Biltmore House, one of Asheville's most notable and most visited attractions, is surrounded by formal and informal gardens, plus 8,000 acres of forest, fields, and farms crisscrossed with paved and unpaved trails. ♿ *activity dependent*

Although most people think about the amazing mansion when they think of Biltmore, an array of available outdoors activities include the following. **Hiking:** 22 miles of hiking trails are available, ranging from easy to moderately challenging, plus more than 2 miles of paths through the gardens. **Biking:** Bring your own bike or rent bikes on-site. Bike paths are level and approachable for all riders. Off-road trails are open to mountain bikers. **Horseback Riding:** Horses are provided, and all rides are guided. **Fly-fishing:** Take a 2-hour or half-day fly-fishing course, or try a guided fly-fishing tour in a drift boat. **Water Sports:** Raft trips (guided), stand-up paddleboard (SUP) trips (guided), and kayak trips (self-guided) are available. **Land Rover Rentals:** Learn how to off-road, drive a short obstacle course, or spend some time on the trails.

Located less than 10 miles from central Asheville, the Blue Ridge Parkway provides access to dozens of miles of hiking trails.

Difficulty: Moderate

Length/Time: 1.2 miles, with access to additional trails; 1-2 hours

Hours/Fees: 9 a.m.-5 p.m. daily (portions of the parkway may be closed during inclement weather, so check website for closings); Free

Getting There: *199 Hemphill Knob Rd. (BRP milepost 384)*
GPS: N35° 33.9484', W82° 29.1793'

Contact: 828-298-5330; blueridgeheritage.com/attractions-destinations/blue-ridge-parkway-visitor-center

Additional Information: A 1.2-mile, moderate loop trail begins at the Blue Ridge Parkway (BRP) Headquarters parking lot. The same loop connects to the Mountains-to-Sea Trail (marked with white blazes), which tracks parallel to the Parkway from Craggy Gardens to Mount Pisgah. You can access the Mountains-to-Sea Trail at many points along the BRP, including the Folk Art Center (milepost 382) and the Rattlesnake Lodge Trail (trip 16). ♿

The BRP meanders 469 miles through the Appalachian Mountains, from Great Smoky Mountains National Park to Shenandoah National Park. The entire length of the Parkway is excellent for cycling. Be prepared for long and strenuous climbs. For the best long-range views, begin at the NC 191 entry to the Parkway and ride south (toward Mount Pisgah); or begin at Craven Gap and ride toward Mount Mitchell (25 miles to the north). Bikes should have head- and taillights, as there are several tunnels in both directions. Mountain bikes are not allowed on trails adjacent to the Parkway.

BOTANICAL GARDENS AT ASHEVILLE AND GLENN'S CREEK GREENWAY

Five minutes from the middle of the city, these gardens offer gentle walking paths through 10 acres of native habitat.

Difficulty: Easy to Moderate

Length/Time: Approximately 1 mile; 1-2 hours

Hours/Fees: Sunrise-sunset daily; Free (donations appreciated)

Getting There: *151 W.T. Weaver Blvd.* GPS: N35° 36.7487', W82° 33.9609'

Contact: 828-252-5190; ashevillebotanicalgardens.org

Additional Information: The Southern Appalachian Mountains boast one of the world's most diverse temperate ecosystems. The Botanical Gardens includes more than 600 species native to the region, including more than 50 considered to be uncommon, rare, or endangered. The approximately half-mile path through the gardens crosses two small streams—Glenn's Creek and Reed Creek—and includes both woodland and meadow habitats. A stroll through the gardens is a quick, relaxing retreat and a refreshing dose of nature. ♿

Nearby Glenn's Creek Greenway is a 0.9-mile (each way) asphalt path linking the Botanical Gardens to Weaver Park, and it's perfect for running, biking, or sightseeing. If you're looking for a quick getaway close to downtown, this area near the University of North Carolina Asheville fills the bill.

No pets are allowed in the gardens, but leashed dogs are welcome on the Greenway.

Located 10 minutes from central Asheville on the French Broad River, this site is replete with active outdoor opportunities.

Difficulty: Easy

Length/Time: Up to 3 miles; 1-3 hours

Hours/Fees: 6 a.m.-10 p.m. daily; Free

Getting There: *220 Amboy Rd.* GPS: N35° 33.9762', W82° 34.7177'

Contact: ashevillenc.gov/civicax/filebank/blobdload.aspx?BlobID=23596

Additional Information: Along with the expected park amenities—picnic areas, a large playground, open areas to throw a Frisbee or soak up the sun—you'll find a dog park, roller-hockey rink, volleyball and basketball courts, and baseball and soccer fields. You'll also find a wide, level, mostly paved pathway for walking, running, and biking. A 1-mile loop of trail runs within the park. ♿

Expanding what is already one of Asheville's most popular recreation areas, the 2.83-mile French Broad River Greenway connects Carrier Park to both Hominy Creek Park and the French Broad River Park in West Asheville. The pedestrian- and bike-friendly Greenway exits the western edge of Carrier Park, follows the French Broad River, and offers views of Biltmore Estate.

Carrier Park is also home to Asheville's only velodrome. Dubbed the "Mellowdrome" by locals, the gently banked, 500-meter asphalt was once the popular Asheville Motor Speedway. The track is open to cyclists of every age and skill. Regular, scheduled bike races attract lively crowds of spectators.

CRAGGY GARDENS

Approximately 20 miles from Asheville, enjoy scenic hikes through forests of rhododendron and mountain laurel, with expansive views.

Difficulty: Moderate to Difficult, depending on route

Length/Time: 2 miles (approximately 1 hour, out and back) for Craggy Gardens Trail; up to 5 hours to Douglass Falls (round-trip)

Hours/Fees: Trails open sunrise-sunset, with Visitor Center open Memorial Day-October (may be closed during inclement weather); Free

Getting There: *Blue Ridge Parkway, Milepost 364.1.* GPS: N35° 42.0162', W82° 22.7782'

Contact: blueridgeheritage.com/attractions-destinations/craggy-gardens

Additional Information: Not only a preferred locale in the Asheville area, Craggy Gardens is a favorite spot along the entire Blue Ridge Parkway. From the Craggy Gardens Visitor Center, the 2-mile, out-and-back Craggy Gardens Trail crosses high-elevation, wildflower-covered balds with groves of rhododendrons and gnarled trees. The strenuous hike to 70-foot-high Douglass Falls descends for 4 miles, with a return on the same route. Bathrooms and refreshments are available at the Visitor Center.

The Craggy Gardens Pinnacle Trail starts at a parking lot located north of the Visitor Center and climbs 250 feet to a rocky, 5,900-foot summit with 360-degree views to Mount Mitchell (the highest peak in the eastern United States) and all the way to Tennessee. This short, 1.4-mile round-trip hike is moderate, with some steep sections. Near the Pinnacle, a side trail leads to lower overlooks. If you start your day in downtown Asheville, remember that it may be considerably cooler at Craggy Gardens due to the elevation.

DuPont State Forest, an hour's drive from Asheville, is home to gorgeous waterfalls and more than 80 miles of trails.

Difficulty: Moderate (most popular waterfall hikes) to Difficult (Cedar Rock and Big Rock Trails)

Length/Time: 3 miles for popular waterfall views; 3-5 hours

Hours/Fees: 5 a.m.-10 p.m. daily; Free (donations appreciated)

Getting There: *1300 Staton Rd., Cedar Mountain.* GPS: N35° 11.5753', W82° 36.2886'

Contact: dupontforest.com

Additional Information: A 3-mile loop, beginning at the Hooker Falls Access, includes three of the forest's six waterfalls: Hooker Falls, Triple Falls, and High Falls. Or, begin at the High Falls parking area, which has a Visitor Center and bathrooms.

A 7-mile loop passes High Falls, Triple Falls, Bridal Veil Falls, and Lake Juliana. Cedar Rock and Big Rock trails traverse the granite "slickrock" that covers much of Cedar Rock Mountain. Easiest access is from the Corn Mill Shoals Parking lot. Cyclists should check out Ridgeline Trail for a smooth, thrilling descent. The trails become narrower and more technical away from the popular waterfall hikes, and trails are open to all users (hikers, bikers, and equestrians), in either direction. ♿ *Limited*

DuPont is popular with equestrians. Shoal Creek Farm (adjacent to DuPont Forest) and others offer guided trail rides.

If you venture beyond the popular waterfall hikes, a trail map (available at local bookstores, bike shops, and outfitters) is recommended.

LAKE POWHATAN

Featuring a small beach with swimming, a fishing pier, picnic areas, and changing and restroom facilities, Lake Powhatan also offers access to miles of trails, perfect for hiking, biking, and enjoying nature.

Difficulty: Easy to Difficult. The trails immediately surrounding Lake Powhatan are an easy hike. The trails become more technically challenging, and the climbs steeper, as you ascend into the surrounding mountains.

Length/Time: More than 40 miles of trails are available; at least 2 hours

Hours/Fees: Lake Powhatan Campground is open March-November and offers tent pads, picnic tables, hot showers, and available electric hookups; Lake access, $2 per person

Getting There: *375 Wesley Branch Rd.* GPS: N35° 29.5102', W82° 37.1622'

Contact: 828-670-5627; recreation.gov/camping/lakepowhatan/r/campgroundDetails.do?contractCode=NRSO&parkId=70206

Additional Information: Both Homestead Trail and Small Creek Trail, which together encircle Lake Powhatan, intersect with Hard Times Road, a doubletrack that provides access to all of Bent Creek's hiking and biking opportunities. Or follow Hard Times Road for more than 2,000 feet of climbing to reach the Blue Ridge Parkway. A few clearly marked trails are closed to bikes. The trails offer limited long-range views, but the lush and densely wooded forest, crisscrossed by mountain streams, is home to deer, bears, horned owls, and many species of flora and fauna unique to the southern Appalachians. ♿ *Limited*

With Lake Powhatan's proximity to Bent Creek Experimental Forest (trip 4) just a few miles from downtown Asheville, you can combine the two locations for a full day of outdoor activities.

Located 15 minutes from downtown Asheville, this is a popular paddling destination, as well as a hub for cyclists who are looking to enjoy a scenic road ride without extended climbs.

Difficulty: Moderate to Difficult

Length/Time: Up to 40 miles (or more) of road biking; 1 or more hours

Hours/Fees: Sunrise-sunset daily; Free

Getting There: *1080 Old Marshall Hwy., Alexander.* GPS: N35° 41.0708', W82° 37.0499'

Contact: buncombecounty.org/Governing/Depts/Parks/Facilities/River/Ledges.aspx

Additional Information: For paddlers, Ledges Park offers easy put-ins and take-outs, a flat approach, and a 200-yard run of class I/II rapids with several play spots, including holes, small waves, and movable gates to practice your slalom technique or improve your water skills. Advanced paddlers may attain (paddle upstream) for a greater workout. If you have more time (and a way to shuttle), you can paddle or float downriver 5 miles and take out at Walnut Island River Park.

Ledges Park makes a great starting point for cyclists looking for an out-and-back ride along the French Broad River. Ride south on Old Marshall Highway into Asheville's River Arts District, or head downstream (keep the river on your left) for an 18-mile ride into historic Marshall in Madison County.

Ledges River Park is also a great place to enjoy a picnic, wade into the waters of the French Broad, or cast a fishing line.

MOUNT PISGAH TRAIL

A popular, moderately difficult, out-and-back hike of just more than 2 miles to the 5,700-foot peak of Mount Pisgah.

Difficulty: Moderate with a Difficult finish near the peak

Length/Time: 2.2 miles to summit; 2 hours

Hours/Fees: Sunrise-sunset daily (portions of the Blue Ridge Parkway may be closed during inclement weather); Free

Getting There: *Blue Ridge Parkway milepost 407.6.* GPS: N35° 24.9378', W82° 44.9214'

Contact: blueridgeparkway.org/v.php?pg=115

Additional Information: The Mount Pisgah Trail begins at the back of the Mount Pisgah parking area, located at mile marker 407.6, off the Blue Ridge Parkway. A television transmission tower caps the mountain, and the summit is visible from the parking area. In fact, this is one of the more notable summits visible from downtown Asheville.

You will ascend more than 700 feet through a lush hardwood forest in just over a mile. The final half of the trail is particularly steep and rocky, but panoramic, summit views of Pisgah National Forest, Cold Mountain, Fryingpan Mountain, and Looking Glass Rock make the effort worthwhile.

For a longer hike with equally stunning views, take the 6-mile out-and-back trip to Fryingpan Mountain Lookout Tower, a 70-foot-tall fire lookout tower. From the Mount Pisgah parking area, begin on the Mount Pisgah Trail and turn left at the marked trail intersection. The trail runs parallel to the Blue Ridge Parkway, passing the Pisgah Inn and Mount Pisgah Campground. Parking and trail access are free.

Just 30 minutes from downtown Asheville you'll find guided treetop and zipline tours in a natural setting.

Difficulty: Moderate

Length/Time: At most 1.5 miles of hiking; three tours available, ranging from 2 hours to all day in length

Hours/Fees: Open daily (reservations required, so call or book online); Per person, $99 and up

Getting There: *242 Poverty Branch Rd., Barnardsville.* GPS: N35° 47.8169', W82° 26.4454'

Contact: 855-628-4828; navitat.com/asheville-nc/

Additional Information: The Moody Cove Adventure features 10 ziplines, ranging in height from 10 to 200 feet off the ground. Platforms between ziplines are built in the trees, allowing for beautiful views and a unique perspective on the surrounding forest. The tour includes two rappels and three short, easy hikes, totaling approximately 0.35 mile.

The Blue Ridge Experience is designed to thrill, offering the longest (up to 3,600 ft.), highest (more than 350 feet above the ground), and fastest (up to 65 mph) ziplines in the area. This tour takes you from peak to peak, providing amazing views, and includes four easy-to-moderate hikes, totaling just more than a mile.

The "Ultimate" package includes both tours and lasts approximately 7 hours.

Participants must weigh a minimum of 70 pounds, and closed-toed shoes are required.

NORTH CAROLINA ARBORETUM

This famed arboretum features 65 acres of carefully tended gardens (including a much-loved Bonsai exhibit and the National Native Azalea Repository) and greenhouses, surrounded by natural forest.

Difficulty: Easy to Moderate

Length/Time: Up to 10 miles of hiking paths, with access to 40+ miles of additional trails for hiking and biking; at least 2 hours

Hours/Fees: Hours vary seasonally, but generally are 8 a.m.-sundown; Parking fees: cars, $12; RVs (21 feet or larger), $50; buses, $100

Getting There: *100 Frederick Law Olmsted Way.* GPS: N35° 29.8711', W82° 36.4944'

Contact: 828-665-2492; ncarboretum.org

Additional Information: Perched at the entrance to the Blue Ridge Parkway where it crosses the French Broad River, the North Carolina Arboretum is an easy 20-minute drive from Asheville. In addition to walking paths that explore the gardens and special exhibits, there are nearly 10 miles of hiking and biking trails, ranging from easy to moderately challenging (garden and trail maps are available at the Arboretum buildings or online). 🚻

Bent Creek Road (for cyclists) and Bent Creek Trail (foot traffic only) run parallel to Bent Creek for more than a mile, making for a flat, relaxing ride or walk. For those seeking greater challenges, Owl Ridge Trail meets Hard Times Road, which allows access to Bent Creek Experimental Forest (trip 4), Lake Powhatan (trip 11), and other areas within the more than half-million acres of Pisgah National Forest.

This hike offers two different approaches through a dense hardwood forest and ends at the remains of a derelict summer home.

Difficulty: Moderate to Difficult

Length/Time: 1-3 miles, depending on route; 2 hours

Hours/Fees: Sunrise-sunset daily; Free

Getting There: *Ox Creek Rd., Weaverville or Blue Ridge Parkway at Tanbark Ridge Tunnel (mile marker 374.4).* From downtown Asheville, take I-240 to Exit 4A, US 19/23N. Go to Exit 21 and turn right at the end of the ramp, followed by an immediate left. In 0.8 mile, turn right onto Reems Creek Rd. In 4 miles, turn right onto Ox Creek Rd. The parking area is a small pull-off on the left, in 3.5 miles. GPS: N35° 40.1068', W82° 27.3408'

Contact: rattlesnakelodge.com/maps.htm

Additional Information: Rattlesnake Lodge was the summer home of Dr. Chase P. Ambler and his family. Built in 1904, it burned in 1926. The foundations of a swimming pool, barn, springhouse, and toolshed remain.

There are two approaches to the lodge. From the parking area on Ox Creek Rd., turn left where the trail splits and ascend a series of switchbacks on the Mountains-to-Sea Trail, following the white blazes. This 1.5-mile moderate hike has rocky sections. As you approach the lodge, you'll see the remains of the swimming pool on the right. An information board marks the site and provides some history.

The hike from Tanbark Ridge Tunnel on the Blue Ridge Parkway is shorter (0.5 mile) but steeper and more difficult. At the summit, a large fallen oak marks the location of the springhouse.

Set within scenic Reems Creek Valley, this historic site re-creates the Vance homestead around original stonework, with a five-room log house surrounded by six outbuildings furnished in the style of the early 1800s.

Difficulty: Easy

Length/Time: Less than a mile; a mild walk to explore the grounds will take an hour or less.

Hours/Fees: 9 a.m-5 p.m. Tuesday-Saturday, with guided tours hourly 9:30 a.m.-4:30 p.m.; Free (donations appreciated)

Getting There: *911 Reems Creek Rd., Weaverville.* GPS: N35° 42.0587', W82° 29.7759'

Contact: 828-645-6706; nchistoricsites.org/vance/

Additional Information: Zebulon Baird Vance—for whom the Vance Monument in downtown Pack Square is named—was a military officer and longtime politician on both the state and federal levels. He is perhaps best known as North Carolina's Civil War governor but was later known as a distinguished U.S. Senator. His birthplace, located approximately 12 miles from downtown Asheville, is now a re-created pioneer farmstead and is open for tours. An on-site Visitor Center details Vance's life and career while offering a glimpse into rural life in the 1800s. ♿

The Vance Birthplace, near the wonderful small town of Weaverville, is also just 5 miles from the Rattlesnake Lodge trailhead (trip 16) and access to the Blue Ridge Parkway at Bull Gap (milepost 376.6)—making it easy to combine activities if you have more time. Craggy Gardens and Mount Mitchell (the highest point in the United States east of the Mississippi) lie to the north, along the Parkway (mileposts 364.4 and 355.4, respectively).

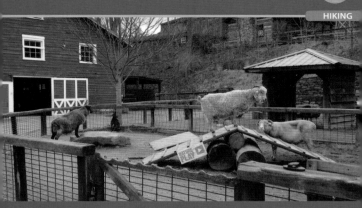

A 15-minute drive from Pack Square, this site is home to more than 60 animal species, including river otters, black bears, cougars, and coyotes.

Difficulty: Easy to Moderate

Length/Time: Approximately 2 miles; 2-3 hours

Hours/Fees: 10 a.m.-5 p.m. daily, except Thanksgiving, Christmas Eve, Christmas Day, and New Year's Day; Adults, $10.95; Seniors (ages 65 and up), $9.95; Ages 3-15, $6.95. No pets allowed.

Getting There: *75 Gashes Creek Rd.* GPS: N35° 34.5648', W82° 29.7758'

Contact: 828-259-8080; wncnaturecenter.com

Additional Information: Owned by the City of Asheville and with a history dating back to the 1920s, the WNC Nature Center allows visitors to set their own pace while connecting with nature.

A graded, paved walking path meanders through the Center's 42 acres, past great horned owls and red-tailed hawks, white-tailed deer, and endangered red wolves. In the Appalachian Station, catch a glimpse of the rare hellbender salamander, a native of the Southern Appalachians and the largest aquatic salamander in the United States. For those who like to get up close with the animals, there's a miniature farmyard with a petting area and daily animal programs. There are also several play areas for children to slide, climb, and build. ♿

For more adventures, the Trillium Glen Nature Trail, a mild, 0.7-mile hiking path through deciduous hardwood forest, leads to views of the Swannonoa River.

WOODFIN RIVERSIDE PARK

Located less than 5 miles from Pack Square, this riverside park offers access to the French Broad River with a kayak/canoe launch, plus fishing, paved walking paths, bathrooms, open areas, and a picnic shelter with grills (bring your own charcoal).

Difficulty: Easy (walking trails) to Difficult (paddling)

Length/Time: Approximately 0.5 mile of walking trails; 1-3 hours

Hours/Fees: Sunrise-sunset daily; Free

Getting There: *1630 Riverside Dr., Woodfin.* GPS: N35° 37.8790', W82° 36.0034'

Contact: woodfin-nc.gov/parks.htm

Additional Information: Woodfin Riverside Park, part of a growing recreation corridor along Riverside Drive, is a perfect put-in for paddlers. Park your shuttle approximately 5 miles away at Ledges Whitewater River Park (trip 12), or continue for a total of 7 miles and take out at Alexander Bridge. There is an unrunnable diversion dam downstream from the put-in. It's best to carry the dam on the left. ♿

Woodfin Riverside Park is also a great starting point for cyclists. Ride south into Asheville's bike-friendly River Arts District and the adjacent Murray Hill Park (with the river on your right, go 4.7 miles on Riverside Drive, turn right on Lyman Street, and right again on Depot Street). Or ride north along the French Broad River toward Marshall. Both rides are relatively flat, a rarity around Asheville.

A one-stop shop, here you'll find nearly everything you'll need to float down the French Broad River, including deluxe tubes with backrests (and a tube for your cooler, if you like), parking, and a shuttle.

Difficulty: Easy to Moderate

Time: Float times vary, depending on the water level and your own pace, but allow for at least 2 hours on the river.

Hours/Fees: 10 a.m.-3 p.m. daily (You must be off the river by 7 p.m.); Per person, including tube and shuttle, $20 (no reservations necessary/extra charge for cooler tube)

Getting There: Two locations: *608 Riverside Dr.* GPS: N35° 36.2953', W82° 34.6849' and *1648 Brevard Rd.* GPS: N35° 29.7364', W82° 35.4484'

Contact: woodfin-nc.gov/parks.htm

Additional Information: If you're in Asheville on a warm day, a float down the French Broad River is a great way to spend a few relaxing hours while enjoying the great outdoors that helped to put this city on the map. Zen Tubing has two locations: One is 7 minutes from downtown, and the other is in south Asheville.

From the downtown location, you'll float by the River Arts District, with views of the city. The south Asheville location is more "natural." Both sections of the river are calm (no rapids), wide, and shallow. River trips begin with a shuttle ride to the dropoff and end at the parking area. Bring sunscreen, and wear clothes and shoes that you don't mind getting wet.

You must be at least 4 years old to participate; life jackets (provided by Zen Tubing) are required for ages 14 and younger.

Best For . . .

KIDS

1 Adventure Center of Asheville

8 Carrier Park and French Broad River Greenway

18 WNC Nature Center

DOGS

4 Bent Creek Experimental Forest

8 Carrier Park and French Broad River Greenway

16 Rattlesnake Lodge Trial

MOUNTAIN BIKERS

1 Adventure Center of Asheville

4 Bent Creek Experimental Forest

10 DuPont State Forest

CLOSE TO TOWN

2 Asheville Urban Trail Walking Tour

3 Beaver Lake Bird Sanctuary and Lake View Park

7 Botanical Gardens at Asheville and Glenn's Creek Greenway

PLANT LOVERS

5 Biltmore Estate

7 Botanical Gardens at Asheville and Glenn's Creek Greenway

15 North Carolina Arboretum

WHEELCHAIR ACCESS

5 Biltmore Estate

7 Botanical Gardens at Asheville and Glenn's Creek Greenway

15 North Carolina Arboretum

HIKING

6 Blue Ridge Parkway Visitor Center

9 Craggy Gardens

13 Mount Pisgah Trail

MOUNTAIN VIEWS

9 Craggy Gardens

10 DuPont State Forest

13 Mount Pisgah Trail

HOT DAYS

1 Adventure Center of Asheville

11 Lake Powhatan

20 Zen Tubing